ON-THE-COB

Illustrations by Angela Mitson Written by Giles Reed

© 1980 STUDIO PUBLICATIONS (IPSWICH) LIMITED
PUBLISHED BY STUDIO PUBLICATIONS (IPSWICH) LIMITED
32 PRINCES STREET, IPSWICH, SUFFOLK, ENGLAND.

Corny-on-the-Cob is one of the Munch Bunch.

He lives in an old bucket.

Corny loves gardening. But, most of all, he loves to tell corny jokes. Even though the others sometimes wish he wouldn't.

One day, Spud called an important meeting.

"I'm organising a competition for the best sunflower grown in the village. The first prize will be a greenhouse," he announced.

Corny was delighted. He had always wanted a greenhouse. Now he had his big chance!

Wally Walnut, Billy Blackberry and Scruff Gooseberry were also listening to Spud. And, when he'd finished, they had their own little meeting.

"I think we should play a trick on Corny," said Billy.

"Yes, he's sure to win if we don't do something to stop him," said Scruff.

And, between them, they worked out a plan to stop Corny winning the greenhouse.

Corny decided to grow several sunflowers. Then he could enter the best one in the competition.

Three of them grew very well.

Corny was pleased. "One of these is sure to win," he thought to himself.

Just then, Lucy Lemon came walking past Corny's house. "How are your flowers growing, Corny?" she asked.

"Oh, very nicely, thank you," said Corny. "But look out, Lucy! There's a lion behind you!"

"Aaah. Help!" she squealed.

Corny fell about laughing. "Don't worry, it won't hurt you. It's only a dandyLION! It's a joke. Don't you get it?"

But Lucy didn't think it was very funny.

Then Scruff, Billy and Wally came along for a little chat. Or so they said. But really, they had come to spy on Corny's sunflowers.

"I've got a good joke for you, Scruff. Listen," said Corny. "What is green and spikey, and goes up and down, up and down?"

"Oh I don't know, Corny. Surprise me," said Scruff.

"It's easy – a gooseberry in a lift! That's a good one, isn't it?"

They all groaned. Corny's jokes seemed to be getting worse all the time.

When it was dark, Wally, Billy and Scruff decided it was time to play their trick on Corny.

So they crept out and planted weeds in their own plant-pots.

Then, they went to Corny's garden and swapped their weeds for his lovely sunflowers.

"Now one of us is sure to win," said Wally in his big, loud voice.

"Shhh! Corny might hear us!" said Billy.

First thing the next morning, Corny went out to see how his sunflowers were growing.

He was horrified when he saw them. They had shrivelled and shrunk overnight.

What a disaster! Now he didn't have a chance of winning that lovely greenhouse.

Corny felt very miserable.

Just then, Professor Peabody came along and Corny told him all about the disaster.

Now, Professor Peabody is very clever, and he knows about lots of things. "Why don't you try singing to your plants?" he suggested. "Sometimes it works. I read about it in a book once."

Corny decided to give it a try. But he wasn't sure about singing to the plants himself. "I can't see that working," he thought. "Not with my terrible voice, anyway."

So, he asked the Banana Bunch to sing to them instead.

But it didn't make any difference to the drooping flowers.

Wally Walnut saw the Banana Bunch singing to the weeds. He couldn't wait to get back and tell the others.

They thought it was hilarious.

"Whoever heard of a bunch of bananas singing to a load of weeds?" chuckled Billy.

But Corny didn't give up.

He asked Pedro Orange to sing to his drooping sunflowers.

Now, as you know, Pedro comes from Spain. So, he sang a sunny flower-song to the plants, in Spanish.

Suddenly, one of the plants started to grow and GROW and GROW . . .

Soon, it was the day of the competition.

And everyone was there, waiting for the judging to begin. Except for Corny.

Wally, Billy and Scruff were there. They were entering the sunflowers which they'd stolen from Corny. But they had forgotten to water them, so they looked terrible.

"Where is Corny? Surely he's entering the competition!" said Lizzie Leek.

Wally, Billy and Scruff nudged each other and laughed. They knew. Or at least they thought they did.

Suddenly, in walked a huge sunflower. The Munch Bunch could hardly see Corny staggering behind it. Everyone gasped. Corny had done it again!

"However does he do it?" asked Casper Carrot. "He must have green fingers!"

But only Corny and Pedro knew the truth. You see, one of the weeds that Billy and the others had given Corny was really a sleepy sunflower. And, when it heard Pedro's sunny song, it woke up and started to grow very quickly.

But Corny didn't tell them that.

He let them all go on thinking
that it was his green fingers
which had done the trick.